Indian Palmistry

Indian Palmistry

J. B. Dale

BLUEJAY

Bluejay Books Pvt. Ltd.
A-8/76, Ist Floor, Sector 16
Rohini, Delhi 110 085
Email: info@bluejaybooksindia.com

First published in 2013 by
Bluejay Books Pvt. Ltd.

Typeset at Bluejay

Printed and bound in India

Contents

Preface

Cheiromancy, the art of foretelling the events of life by the lineaments of the hand, derived its name from the Greek word *cheiros*, the plam, and *manteia,* to foretell, whence it has been vulgarly called Palmistry—as it is named in a recent Act of Parliament to forbid its practice for gain or reward. In Coleman's *Mythology of the Hindoos,* p. 202, it is written: "On the Buddha's foot is the mark called the 'chakravarti,' wheel or discus, which should have been on the palm of the hand, by which the sages at his birth divined that he would rise to considerable eminence." He says (p. 19): "Various data have been assigned to the period of Buddha's existence. The most correct seems to be about 550 B.C., whence, as the sages practised cheiromancy at Buddha's birth, its existence must have been much earlier known among the Indians." "In the year 1652," writes Zadkiel, "the celebrated astrologer, Geo. Wharton, Esq., published a translation of 'a matchless piece' as he terms it, on the subject, written in Latin by Dr. J. Rothman." Since that period the art of cheiromancy has gradually fallen into disuse, chiefly from the extensive nonsense published by recent writers. One of the writers makes a shallow attempt to disprove the connection which exists between astrology and palmistry, while another says it is based on the principles of the Kabalah, the latter being nothing more than a mnemonical system of astrology. From the writings of Dr. J. Rothman and Geo. Wharton, Esq., I propose now to give, together with some of the choicest of those of the East, the principal matter, and to explain in the ordinary language used by palmisters such points as may require elucidation. Mr. Wharton, a careful student in these subjects, clearly proves that palmistry can only act in accordance with astrology, and that the art of cheiromancy cannot be relied upon beyond the period of one to two years at most, for he observes in his preface, "What more convincing than if, by inspection made into the hand of any man, I truly pronounce this or that planet essentially dignified or angular in his geniture, or in such or such a position with other planets or stars, another unfortunate, afflicted or defected? Or if, on the contrary, by looking first into the geniture and considering therein the several positions of the planets and their configurations one to another and with other stars, I tell him, and that distinctly and truly, the lines and signatures engraven upon his head or hand—what, I say, is or can be more satisfactory than this to rational men, as touching the power and influence of the planets and stars upon these inferiors, and consequently of the lawful use and truth of the science called astrology, cheiromancy and metoposcopy, between which three sciences there appear to be such a secret coherence and harmony?"

It is also written in the *Book of Job,* xxxvii. 7: "In the hand of all men he shall put a mark that everyone may know his own work"; but in our translation of the *Bible* it is written as follows: "In the hand of all men he putteth a mark that every man may know his own work." This alone proves that Job believed in this science.

The author does not claim that there is anything new in this work, although the method of translating and setting may be original.

The Reference Hand

References to Hand

1

Name – Mount of Jupiter.

Location – Root of forefinger.

Interpretation – When very fully shown denotes pride, tyranny; when deficient in size denotes idleness and vulgarity; when there are concentric circles shown by the pores of the skin, they indicate sure success in religion, marriage and monetary matters, ambition; broken circles or elongated, slightly less powerful; entirely void, no success thereby.

Name – Mount of Saturn.

Location – Root of middle finger.

Interpretation – When fully marked denotes wisdom, predence; when very full, taciturnity, sadness; when concentric circles are placed, success in all Saturnian affairs; when absent or elongated, the person will never make much headway with such things and persons.

3

Name – Mount of the Sun, "Apollo".

Location – Root of ring finger.

Interpretation – When prominent it gives art, genius, intelligence; when very full, denotes a greedy and untruthful disposition; when flat or small, it causes the person to be dull; when concentric circles appear here, the person will be very powerful, have riches and honor by the state, or marry a high-born person; elongated or none, shows the person will have mean preferment, or none, as the case may be.

4

Name – Mount of Mercury.

Location – Root of little finger.

Interpretation – When prominent and full, and with concentric circles thereon, it denotes science, inventiveness, wit and success in all Mercurial matters, as writings, professions, especially church and law, and journeys; when very large and with elongated circles, it denotes theft, lying, cunning; when flat or none, it shows a negative life, and unfortunate in all above.

5

Name – Girdle of Venus.

Location – A curved line from root of forefinger to root of little finger.

Interpretation – When this line is clear it shows a natural desire for the opposite sex; when double it denotes an intemperate and lustful life; when broken, it show terrible loss and infamy through lusts, a filthy person.

Name – Via Combusta.

Location – Extends through hollow of hand to mount of middle finger.

Interpretation – See Lines (8) page 36.

Name – Via Solis.

Location – A curved line running from root of ring finger to the mount of the Moon.

Interpretation – When straight, uniformly composed and well-coloured, it promises the favour of great men and great honours; if dissected or uneven judge the contrary, or the frowns or ill favour of great people, with impediments in life, or envy.

Name – Line of Fortune.

Location – A line extending from the mount of Jupiter to the mount of Mercury.

Interpretation – When long and with incisures, denotes that the principal members of the body are strong, constancy; if short or crooked, the contrary; if severed, the same; when it stops at the mount of Saturn, it shows a vain, lying person; if it branches on mount of Jupiter it denotes honours; if single or without branches, it shows poverty and want.

9

Name – Liver line.

Location – A curved line running through the palm of the hand, between the line of Fortune and the Life line.

Interpretation – When straight and not dissected by obscure little lines, denotes a healthy body; if extending only to the hollow of the hand, or short, it denotes a short life, or full of disease; the longer this line, the longer may the life be; if cut at end, poverty in old age.

10

Name – Line of Life.

Location – A curved line running round the root of the thumb.

Interpretation – When broad and uniform, denotes a long and healthy life, and but few diseases; if slender, short or cut, or with little obscure lines running through, it denotes feebleness of body, sickness, short life, except line be strong; if sloping nicely to Liver line, and beautified in the angle with parallels or little crosses, it shows a good wit and even temper.

11

Name – Line of Saturn.

Location – A line extending from the wrist lines up to middle finger.

Interpretation – If it extends to the middle finger it indicates profound meditations, and if fortunate, events in counsels and actions; if short (without other testimony), misfortunes; if bent towards the mount of the Moon, in the hollow of the hand, imprisonment.

12

Name – Line of the Head and Brain, called by some the line of Health.

Location – A line running from the wrist, or line of Saturn, and extending up to the mount of Mercury.

Interpretation – If this line be uniform and not intersected, it forms with the line of Life and Liver line (sometimes called the Head line) a triangle on the plane of Mars. If of good colour, it denotes prudence, manly wit and fair fortune; the more perfect this triangle, the better will be the person's wit and courage; if obtuse, it shows an evil nature and a rude man; no triangle shows a fool or a knave.

13

Name – Line of the Moon.

Location – A line running from the line of Saturn and line of the Brain to the mount of the Moon, sometimes called the Via Lacteal.

Interpretation – This line being uniformly composed, proportionate and continued, denotes fortunate journeys both by land and sea; also a good brain, the favour of women (the mount of Venus being also unaffiliated), a composed and graceful speech; if it be cut or distorted, it argues infelicity and proneness to lies; if whole and ascending up to little finger, it denotes great happiness.

14

Name – Mount of the Moon.

Location – The outside part of hand, opposite to root of thumb, between mount of Mercury and wrist.

Interpretation – Imagination, refinement, poetry; if very large or full, it denotes despair, caprice and almost lunacy; when flat and hollow, denotes dulness, want of speech, positiveness.

15

Name – Plane and place of Mars. The mount of Mars.

Location – The place of Mars is twice represented, one on the side of the palm by the mount of Mars, and the other in the palm between the line of Life and the Liver line, called the plane or place of Mars.

Interpretation – The mount of Mars shows courage; when in excess, passion; when small, temerity.

(*Vide* marks, etc., specially numbered).

16

Name – Mount of Venus.

Location – In the root of the thumb.

Interpretation – Love of beauty and pleasure; where large, inconstancy, coquetry; when small, coldness.

17

Name – Dragon lines or Bracelets.

Location – Lines to be found on the wrist.

Interpretation – If double or triple and forming a right and continuous tract, it shows good composure of body; thrice, indicates health, wealth and prosperity; a star or cross here shows tranquillity in old age; if a line extends to the mount of Moon or Mercury from Dragon lines, it shows esteem and life in a foreign country.

18

Name – Plane of Mensa, or place of Fortune.

Location – The space between the line of Fortune and the Liver line.

Interpretation – Great and broad, forming a nice figure, it declares a liberal man, magnanimous and long-lived; if small and narrow, it argues slender fortune, niggardliness and fearfulness; a star or cross in this space, clear and well-proportioned, especially under the mount of the Sun, shows honours and dignities to follow.

19

Name – Egyptian Staff.

Location – Just below chain of Fortune.

Interpretation – Great renown in antiquities—a great commander and ofttimes a great statesman, a lover of ancient research.

20

Name – Chain of Fortune.

Location – Small crosses or stars between the line of Life and the Liver line, under the mount of Jupiter.

Interpretation – These denote wit and an even nature; riches and honours, or wealth by position of noted kind.

21

Name – Sun place.

Location – A small circle on the line of Life, opposite to the mount of Moon.

Interpretation – The loss of eyesight; two circles, the loss of both eyes.

22

Name – Envy line.

Location – A line running from the root of the thumb, near the Dragon lines, to the line of Saturn.

Interpretation – Denotes envy.

23

Name – Perilous line.

Location – A small line running from the Life line and passing through the point formed by the cutting of line of Saturn and Liver line.

Interpretation – This indicates perils of all kinds, and disease, and sometimes sudden death or misfortune.

24

Name – Line of Friendship.

Location – A small line starting from the line of Life, about midway, and passing through the Saturn and Liver lines, forming a small triangle, and extending to the mount of Sun.

Interpretation – This shows honours and favours from great ladies of rank and fortune.

25

Name – Cross of Indigence.

Location – A star on the Liver line or natural mean, near or on mount of Moon.

Interpretation – Poverty in old age.

26

Name – Path of Mars.

Location – A small line running midway from line of Life to plane of Mars, with a small star on or near the end.

Interpretation – Hurts and wounds.

27

Name – Dragon's Head.

Location – A star on Dragon line or Bracelets.

Interpretation – Tranquility in life, old age.

28

Name – Dragon's Tail.

Location – A line running from second Bracelet into the mount of Venus.

Interpretation – Adversities from kindred of wife.

29

Name – Line of Mars.

Location – A line running parallel with the line of Life on mount of Venus.

Interpretation – This augments and strengthens the things signified by the line of Life; it particularly promises good success in war and a robust constitution.

30

Name – Mars Cross.

Location – Cross or star on the mount of Mars.

Interpretation – Fortunate journeys.

31

Name – Oracle of Jove.

Location – The sign Jupiter under the mount or on the mount of Apollo.

Interpretation – Denotes honours and ecclesiastical dignities.

32

Name. – Line of Calamity.

Location – A small line running from line of Life up through second joint of thumb.

Interpretation – This signifies a violent death and danger from married women.

33

Name – Cross bars.

Location – Small lines on the second joint of thumb.

Interpretation – This is an indication of contention and brawling; small hair lines running horizontally to thumb shows riches in latter part of life.

34

Name – Girdle of Pollux.

Location.—A ring round the thumb.

Interpretation.—This is an indication of hanging.

35

Name – First phalanx of forefinger.

Location – Small lines running parallel with joint.

Interpretation – Indication of inheritance. This phalanx,

hollow or curved upwards, indicates avarice; if turned backwards, extravagance.

36

Name – Second phalanx of forefinger.

Location – Small lines in the centre, running vertical to joints.

Interpretation – Indicates many children.

37

Name – Third phalanx of forefinger.

Location – Small lines running vertical to joints.

Interpretation – Denotes a jovial disposition. This finger thick at the root denotes a greedy appetite.

38

Name – Small star or cross.

Location – On third phalanx of forefinger.

Interpretation.—Shows an unchaste and lascivious life.

39

Name – Small star.

Location – On second phalanx of middle finger.

Interpretation – Denotes melancholy; a star near middle of third phalanx denotes unhappiness.

40

Name – A line with star at bottom.

Location – A small line running throughout middle finger, with a star on third phalanx.

Interpretation – Denotes folly and madness.

41

Name – Small lines running vertical to joint.

Location – Second phalanx of ring finger.

Interpretation – Indicates fame, especially if a straight and well-defined line passes up the middle of the finger.

42

Name – Small cross bars.

Location – Third phalanx of ring finger.

Interpretation – Honours and riches.

43

Name – Small cross or star.

Location – On mount of Mercury close to joint.

Interpretation – Eloquence.

Name – Two small stars or indented line.

Location – On mount of Mercury, one below the other, or a clear indented line on mount of Apollo.

Interpretation – The first indicates a brilliant mind. The line on mount of Apollo also shows a noted and brilliant mind, but the loss of a dear male friend, sometime death of wife.

Name – Cross bars.

Location – On second phalanx of little finger.

Interpretation – Shows a theif or a very deceitful person.

Name – Marriage lines.

Location – Small lines on outside of hand on mount of Mercury.

Interpretation – These, according to their number, denote the number of husbands or wives should the widow line also appear; without it they may mean lovers.

Name – Crest of Hermes.

Location – Small crosses or star on third phalanx of little finger, especially in the centre.

Interpretation – Shows ingenuity and eloquence.

48

Name – Small concentric circles formed by pores of the skin.

Location – On first phalanx of all fingers.

Interpretation – Denotes that the persons will be always earning or inheriting money all his life, and in fact it is one of the most successful signs in the hand for pecuniary success.

49

Name – On Mounts.

Location – Concentric.

Interpretation – The same on the mounts indicate money by or through persons or things indicated by the mount of the fingers, on the forefinger, a wealthy partner; on the mount of Saturn, wealth by lands, house property, legacies; on the ring finger by successful business, or profession and fame; on the mount of Mercury by writings, profession, eloquence, etc. Should these assume an elongated form, as seen on middle finger, then, if unbroken, the person will succeed by labour and many difficulties; if none appear, then they will never succeed in pecuniary matters, unless the hand is otherwise very strong.

50

Name – Lapis Lazuli.

Location – Tip of middle finger.

Interpretation – Same as above on mount of Saturn, but in foreign countries or from abroad.

51

Name – Lapis Lazuli.

Location – On mount of Saturn or middle finger.

Interpretation – Same as No. 50.

52

Name – Shell form show by pores of skin.

Location – On first phalanx of little finger.

Interpretation – This is perhaps the best means of success, as shown above, in writing and speaking, etc., if other testimonies concur, but I prefer the complete circle.

53

Name – Corn or diamond loops.

Location – On joints of fingers.

Interpretation – Should the lines on the joints, between the phalanges of the fingers, take the form of a barleycorn or diamond, the person may expect many and unexpected advantages, but much depends on the sum of these lines when counted.

54

Name – Luna lines.

Location – Near mount of Moon on outside of hand, below the Liver or Father line.

Interpretation – Aptitude for travelling, a sailor, quietness, contentment, poetic imagination when regular; cross bars here give discontent, sometimes suicide, a morbid imagination.

55

Name – Line of intuition.

Location – A line running from the Liver line to the mount of Moon.

Interpretation – This shows poetic intelligence, seldom found except in highly imaginative and intellectual persons.

56

Name – Line of Temper.

Location – A line running vertically from mount of Mars to mount of Moon.

Interpretation – This denotes determination and decision.

A Summary of Judgment

(1) Observe the kind of hands from the front or inside.

Short hands denote an impulsive judgment without analysis.

Smooth hands denote impression, ability, inspiration, intuition.

Hard, firm hands denote great energy and perseverance.

Soft, loose hands denote a kind of debility or laziness, a disinclination to work.

Knotted hands denote reflection, order, success.

(2) Observe the fingers.

Pointed. – Forefinger (first), intuitive; middle finger (second), frivolous, light-hearted, gay; ring finger (third), artistic, testy, nice, refined; little finger (fourth), eloquent.

Square – Forefinger (first), truthful, cautious; middle finger (second); grave, thoughtful; ring finger (third), reasonable, a thinker; little finger (fourth), judicious.

Spatulated – Forefinger (first), mystic, delighting in occult studies; middle finger (second), morbid, fanciful; ring finger (third), dramatic, sympathetic; little finger (fourth), mechanical.

(3) Look at the nails on the hands.

1 – Narrow, indicate an irritable temper or aspiring spirit.

2 – Round and full, indicate learning and liberal views.

3 – Small, indicate pride, stubbornness, narrowness and bigotry.

4 – Broad and flat, indicate a mild and timorous disposition.

5 – Filbert-shaped, indicate refinement and courteous manners.

Note – When the hand is allowed to open freely, the space between the first and second fingers, farthest apart, denotes independence of action, and if both are very wide apart, originality and self-reliance.

If the thumb inclines inward, avarice; outward, generosity.

(4) Observe the length and depth of the lines.

(5) The quality, whether they are crooked or straight.

(6) Observe whether they touch or cut other lines.

(7) Observe whether they are touched or cut by other lines.

(8) Their place and position.

Note – The lines are sometimes lengthened until certain years of our life, while others are shortened. At one time they may become pale, at another they become notably clear and red. The minor marks, such as are found on the mounts, sometimes quite vanish, and at other times they will assume different shapes and colours. Therefore, the most studious in palmistry cannot attain a complete knowledge of the events of a life at once, because they come and go as nature, or the circumstances of life, change and twist, but can only read for a year or so in advance. These changes are caused, as before stated, by the progressions and changing of the laws relating to nature, of which we are a part.

The hand to examine

The general rule in the East is that the right palm of the male and the left palm of the female ought to be examined. In either case take the hand in which the signs and lines are clearly shown. If they concur in both hands and appear clear and nicely marked they declare a constancy of fortune and health, etc. In the male generally the right hand is the fate hand or the positive hand, that is, events about to happen; while the left denotes the negative or those events which have come to pass or been accomplished by the person, or those just passing away. Judge the converse in the female hands.

Signification of Animals, Flowers and Promiscuous Marks found on the Hand

These are principally formed by the smaller lines running with the pores of the skin. Great care must therefore be taken in determining these forms, because very much depends on their position. The numbers herein referred to have reference to figure of the hand which I have set apart for the express purpose of showing these marks and signs (p. 23).

The first space of the hand near to the mounts is that part which has principally to show the animal passions – lusts and intrigues.

The second space, or the part of the hand between the girdle of Venus and the Table line, deals more specifically with love affairs or the spiritual side, while the former treats more on the physical plane.

The two, therefore, taken together, may be considered the moral region of the hand.

The next space between the Table line and the Liver line may be called the mental and social region.

The one following this may be called the commercial region or the wealth generally of the person.

The space enclosed by the line of Life is the artistic or dramatic region.

The right hand side of the hand separated by the line of Saturn denotes the positive nature, while the left hand portion is the negative or imaginative nature of the individual.

If a flash or a similar figure be found at the root of the hand (No. 1) it signifies great success in the world, riches and many children.

If a lotus flower or like-shaped figure be here, the person, if a female, will be sure to become a great lady, in fact almost a queen. If the same be on a male hand he will be sure to be renowned and great (No. 2).

For a serpent found here or on the wrist just above the Bracelet and near to the line of Saturn, the man will become a great warrior or hero (Nos. 1 and 3).

An octagonal figure placed between the line of Life and the Liver line will cause the person to be burdened with the possession of landed estates (No. 4).

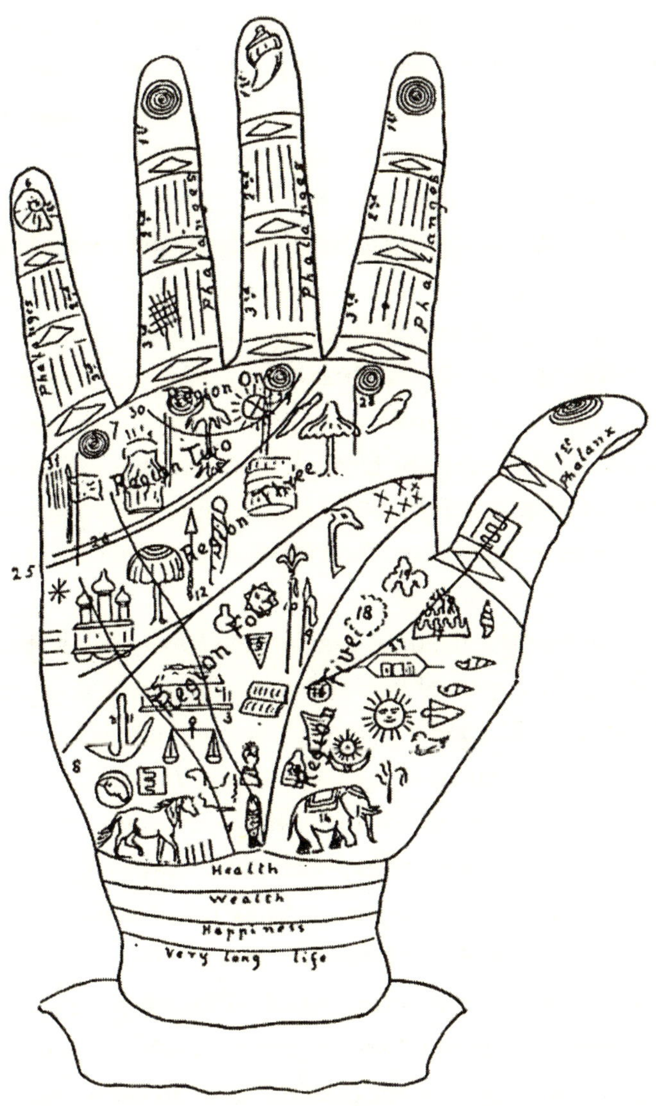
Region One
Region Two
Region Three
Region Four
Region Five
Region
1st Phalanx
Phalanges
Health
Wealth
Happiness
Very long life

If conch, or marine shells, or any circular figure be found here (No. 5) they presage that the person will be a learned man, especially if they should be found on the first phalanx of the little finger (No. 6), on the mount of Mercury (No. 7), or on the mount of the Moon (No. 8).

Should the sign of a flag be found here, and particularly on the mount of Mercury (No. 8) or on the plam of the hand (No. 9), the person will be a philosopher and a great thinker.

A trident (No. 10), the three-pronged sceptre of Nepture or similar figure, the person rises to great fame, almost a prince or princess. If the trident be formed, but somewhat indistinct, he will not rise so high, but sure to have very important appointments and be attached to royalty. He will also be very kind, generous, and likely to acquire fame.

If in the male hand, or even on the female hand, there be anything like a spear or bow and arrow the person is sure to get a throne (No. 11); and if all three, bow, arrow and lance together be there, the person is sure to be a king or queen (No. 12).

Should the sign of a wheel and flag come together on the same hand, the person will have riches and power, respect among his fellow-men, will be a great ruler or prime minister, and be noted or celebrated for his wisdom and goodness (No. 13).

If the sign of an elephant, which of itself is good (No. 14), or the sign of an earring (No. 15) and wheel (No. 16) appear on the same hand together, the person is likely to be an emperor or great personage.

A hill (No. 17) or wristlet (No. 18) like a bough, or something like the head of a man (No. 19), or a pitcher (No. 20), the person is almost sure to rise to the exalted position of a minister of state.

If the sign of a barleycorn be found on the flat part of the thumb, the person will spend life very happily and go through life easily (No. 21). Should the barley appear on the mount of Mars, in the centre of the hand, the person will be very intellectual, respectable and wise (No. 22). Should the form of the barley be found under any two fingers, especially on the mount of Saturn, the possessor will lead a happy life, honorable, have a good partner in marriage and have many children (No. 23).

If the line of Heart (or the line of Fortune in India) (No. 25), extend only to the mount of Apollo (the Sun), the person will scarcely live ten years. And should this line be broken in many places the person will die by drowning. But if another smaller line appears running parallel with the Heart line which extends only to the mount of Apollo (No. 26), the person will meet his death either by a fall from a house or a tree. Should, however, this line extend from the outside part of the hand to the mount of Jupiter, the life will be long and good, if not broken.

If a line rises from mount of Venus to the first phalanx of the thumb, he will be a commander of a large army (No. 27).

A vertical line on the mount of Jupiter, the possessor will be a great diplomatist, but an irreligious person (No. 28). If this line appears on the mount of Saturn, he will be a prosperous man with a beautiful wife and have many children (No. 29).

A line under the Sun denotes a trades person with a long life, but only rises to the middle class (No. 30).

If a vertical and well-defined line appears on the mount of Mercury (No. 31), the person is likely to lead a long life in a foreign country.

If the line of Heart (Fortune line) goes to the mount of Saturn, he will live thirty years.

If the Life line and the Liver line (called the Head line in England) be separated entirely, the female will either be seduced before marriage or have illegitimate children, or in both sexes be illegitimate themselves.

If the palm of the hand be filled with numerous and indistinct marks or lines, the person leads a very unhappy life.

If a person has single lines or marks thus = between the phalanges on the joints of the fingers and when contend together make twelve, they will be happy, prosperous and rich for the most part of life.

If they make thirteen, he will be very unhappy.

If they make fifteen, he will be dishonest or a thief.

If they make seventeen, he will be guilty of debauchery and much wickedness.

If they make eighteen, he will be very clever and respectable.

If they make twenty, an enthusiast in religion.

If they make twenty-one, he will be a great poet and become famous.

When these lines are joined at the ends and form the shape of a barleycorn or wheat, the fame and learning of the person depend on the number; one would be weak, two strong, and so on. If the lines just over the mounts be united at the ends, as described above, the person in whose hands the same appear will have riches and wealth, but generally by marriage. If they be united over all four fingers, the person will be very rich, over three less wealthy and so on.

Small concentric circles, formed principally by the pores of the skin, on the points or first phalanges of the fingers and thumb, and these be not broken and appear same on all four fingers and thumb, the person will be extremely famous and very powerful.

Also on the outer ridge of the hand will be found various marks.

All the marks above the Heart line indicate the number of wives, and all below the number of children, the short one indicates those that will probably die.

The line around the lower joint of the thumb just above the mount of Venus, if well-defined and clear, and particularly if they bend thus ◡ on the mount, denote the person to be famous as a sculptor or painter.

If on the mounts of Jupiter, Saturn, Apollo, Mercury, there be found concentric circles, and very complete, and in no way broken, the man will attain great wealth and power through marriage or marry some noted person.

If at the end of the Hepatica or Liver line there is an opening like the tail of a fish, the person will have great happiness and riches.

The Lines

(1) The line of Life, which ought to be called the line of the Heart, embraces the root of the thumb.

(2) The Liver or natural mean runs straight through the middle of the hand.

(3) The line of the Head or Brain rises before the line of Life and extends towards the mount of Mercury, forming a triangular figure in the palm of the hand – the great sign of success and brilliancy.

(4) The line of Fortune of Title line, which begins under the root of the little finger and extends towards the forefinger.

(5) The Bracelet lines at the root of the hand, stretch across the wrist, and may be single, double or treble, etc.

(6) The Sun line, called for clearness Via Solis, is a right line which begins at the mount of Apollo and stretches into the hollow of the hand after curving towards the mount of Moon.

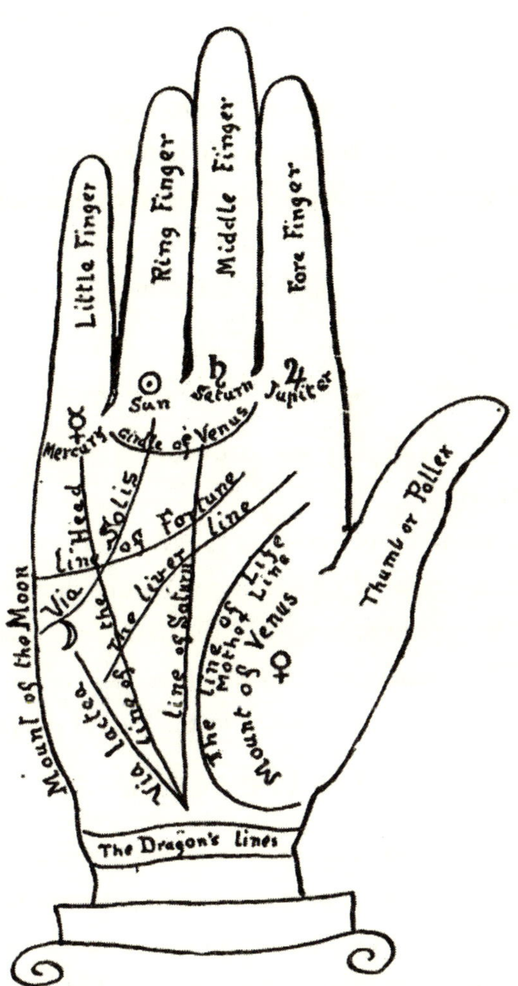

The lines and mounts on the hand

(7) The Line of the Moon, called the Via Lactea, runs upwards from the line of Saturn, through the mount of the Moon.

(8) The line of Fortune or Saturn begins at the wrist lines, extends through the hollow of the hand to the mount of the middle finger. If this line be cut or severed it is called the Via Combusta; when this line assumes a double line in the middle of the palm it is said that you do more good to others than yourself.

The Mounts

These are the fleshy or prominent parts under the fingers, called:

(1) The mount of Venus, in the root of the thumb.

(2) The mount of Jupiter, in the root of the forefinger.

(3) The mount of Saturn, in the root of the middle finger.

(4) The mount of Sun (Apollo), in the root of the ring finger.

(5) The mount of Mercury, in the root of the little finger.

The Line of Life

The line, broad, uniform, lively colour and a good length, denotes the party to be long lived and subject to few diseases. This line slender, short, cut or broken, or with obscure little lines, or pale, or blackish colour, denotes feebleness of body, sickness, short life. When sloping nicely to the Liver line and forming a nice angle with parallel or little crosses at the juncture, shows good wit and even temper, a sharp quick person and business man.

Little branches in the upper part branching towards the Liver line signify riches and honour. These little lines running the opposite way towards the wrist denote poverty, deceit, unfaithful servants. Little confused hairlines in this line signify diseases.

Time of Events

Should they be found in the lower part of the hand, the good or bad will be in early age. In the middle of the hand towards the hollow, in the middle age. If towards the Liver line, in declining age.

Danger of death is threatened if this line be broken.

To find the exact age this line may be divided into seventy parts, each part counting one year of life.

The character ⊙ in this line shows loss of an eye. This character in double denotes the loss of both eyes.

A line ascending from the line of Life (beneath the angle formed by the line of Life and the Liver line) to the line of Saturn, denotes an envious man, and shows also a perilous disease in that part wherein it touches the vital. So much the worse if it cut the line of Life or sever the mount.

A line passing from the line of Life to the ring finger promises honours to follow by means of a lady of rank, or gain through favour.

The line of Life thicker than ordinary at the end under the forefinger shows a laborious old age.

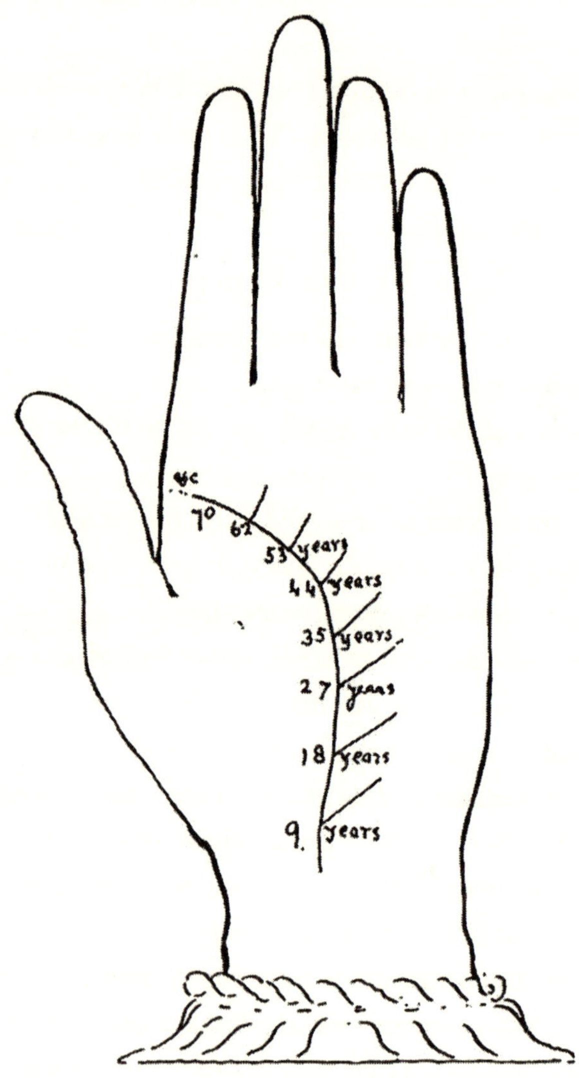

The line of Life

The Liver Line

This line being straight and not dissected by obscure little lines, denotes a healthy body.

If it be short or broken and does not reach beyond the hollow of the hand, it denotes diseases and a short life.

The longer this line, the greater may the life be warranted.

If cut at the end by a small intervening line, it threatens poverty in old age.

When this line is very close to the line of Life, it denotes diseases of the heart, as palpitation, syncope, etc.

If the space between the line of Life and the Liver line, especially of the space between the Liver line and the line of Fortune, be broad, it shows prodigality.

If the Liver line turns and winds several ways, unequal, of a different colour and dissected, it bodes disease or obstruction in the liver, and hence the disease arising from its weakness. It also denotes covetousness and depravity of nature and wit; more especially if from under the region of the middle finger it extends towards the line of Life, thus making a short or narrow triangle. Where it is well-drawn and of a good, clear colour, it is a sign of a cheerful and ingenious disposition.

If this line have a sister line it promises inheritances.

If continued with some little hard knots, it forebodes manslaughter either perpetrated or to be perpertrated, according to the number of those knots.

If a cross be found therein, under the region of the middle finger, it promises death at hand.

If it ends with a fork towards the mount of the Moon, it is a sign of hypocrisy and evil manners.

When it bends towards the Mensal it is a token of a saluderous tongue and envy.

When it projects a remarkable branch through the line of Life unto the mount of Venus, and cuts or touches the line of Mars, especially if the line be of a ruddy colour, it warns to be guarded against thieves and intimates, fraud and deceit of enemies.

This same branch also shows great heat of the liver, coming from Mars, whereby life is endangered.

The Line of the Head and Brain

If this line (ascending from its place with uniform proportion) connect the line of the Liver and Life in a triangular form, having a lively colour and not intersected, it declares a person of admirable prudence, and of a manly wit and fair fortune. The more perfect this triangle, the better shall the temper, wit and courage be. But if it be obtuse, it argues an evil disposed nature and a rude man. If there be no triangle, much worse, a fool, a prodigal and a liar, and frequently a short life.

The nearer it approaches a right angle, and not acute, the better the person. But when the angle formed be very acute, especially when the lines of Liver and Life touch under the region of the middle finger, it argues covetousness. If not under the middle finger, it shows a keen, sharp and powerful will, also a clever business person.

The left angle (male hand), if it be made upon the natural mean in the mount of the Moon, and be a right angle by the line passing to the mount of Mercury, confirms goodness, and quality of the intellect.

When the line of the Head and Brain throws out unequal and incomposed branches towards the mount of the Moon, thereby making unusual characters, it denotes in men weakness of brain and dangerous sea voyages; but in a woman frequent sorrows of mind and difficulties in child-bearing. Equal lines thus projected presage the contrary in both sexes, viz., in men, a clear and well-composed brain and frequent voyages, and in women, cheerfulness and felicity in child-bearing.

The line of the Head has this peculiarity; if it projects a cleft or a manisfest star upwards to the cavea martis, it signifies boldness and courage; but if it let fall the same downwards, thefts and deceitfulness.

When the line of the Head is joined to the line of the Dragon's Head, it promises a prudent and pleasant old age. The same throwing a branch in the shape of a fork towards the place of the line of Fortune signifies subtlety in managing affairs and craftiness, either to do good or evil.

If this character ⊕ appears in or near the fork it gives riches and honours by means of ingenuity and arts.

The Line of Fortune

This line is also called the Table line. This line, when it is long enough and without incisures, argues a due strength in the principal members of man and denotes constancy. Judge the contrary if this line be short or crooked or is severed. When this line terminates under the mount of Saturn, it shows a vain and lying fellow.

If it projects small branches unto the mount of Jupiter, it produces honours. Should this be a simple line on the mount of Jupiter, and void of any good marks or branches, it is a sign of poverty and want.

If it severs the mount of Jupiter, cruelty of mind and excessive wrath.

If it throws a branch between the forefinger and the middle, it threatens to a man a wound in the head, but to a woman danger in child-bearing.

A small line running from the line of Fortune to the space between the middle and ring finger, denotes sorrow and labour.

A line passing from the Liver line to the line of Fortune, forming an acute angle, brings sorrow and labour.

Should there be no Liver line and the line of Fortune connected by a small line to the line of Life, it threatens a deadly wound.

The absence of the line of Fortune shows a malevolent, contentious, faithless, inconstant person of base conditions.

Confused little lines in the line of Fortune denote sickness, and if under Mercury, in the first age; under the mount of the Sun in manhood; under the middle finger in old age.

When certain points are observed in this line, they argue lust and vigour of body.

The Bracelets Line

If this be double or treble and forming a right and continues tract, it promises a good composure of body.

The line which is nearest to the thumb, of a good lively colour, and unbroken, promises riches. Should this line be broken in the middle, crooked and very pale, it denotes debility of body and a want of all things.

A cross or star placed here shows tranquillity of life in old age.

If there be a star, single or double or any line near the mount of the thumb, in women they denote misfortune and infamy.

A line passing from the Dragon line through the mount of Venus, presages adversities either by means of some kindred or a wife.

A line running from the Dragon line to the mount of the Moon shows adversities and private enemies; crooked or distorted, it increases the evil and shows long servitude.

This line being clear and straight and extending as far as the region of the Moon, presages many journeys both by land and sea.

If this line continues to the mount of Mercury it argues that the man will live in a foreign country in great esteem. If it extends to the Liver line it shows an honest behavior and a long life. If to the mount of the Sun, single or double, it denotes great good and enables the man to govern and rule in great affairs. If it passes to the mount of Mercury, it betokens a man fit for many things. If it does not extend to the mount of Mercury, but is broken about the middle and ends beneath that mount, it denotes an untruthful, tittle-tattling, discontented person.

If this line ascends directly to the mount of Saturn, it denotes a good position of Saturn in the geniture; but if crooked and passes towards the Dragon line and the Liver line, it denotes a hard, covetous, and laborious man.

The Via Solis

This line being straight, uniformly composed and well-coloured, promises the favour of great men, and joyful honours; if dissected and uneven, judge the contrary, with various impediments and envy.

The Via Lactea

This line being uniformly composed, proportionate and continued, denotes fortunate journeys both by sea and land; also a good brain, the favour of women (the mount of Venus being unafflicted), a composed and graceful speech. If it be cut or distorted, it argues infelicity and lies; but if whole, ascending towards the little finger, is a sign of great happiness.

The Line of Saturn

This line being fully and wholly protracted to the middle finger is an argument of profound meditations, and of fortunate events in counsels and actions.

This line deficient is an evil sign portending many misfortunes, unless other positions favour it. If bending backward, into the hollow of the hand towards the mount of the Moon, after the form of a semi-circle, threatens imprisonment.

The line beginning from the line of Life and passing through the Liver line, to the mount of Saturn—and if there it touch the Saturnia—threatens imprisonment.

Morality. The Girdle of Venus

This line of itself, unless there be other testimony to counteract it, is sufficient to indicate fullness of nature to appreciate the opposite sex, while the want of it denotes (except in a measure given by the fulness of the mount of Venus, etc.) coldness, unnaturalness for the other sex, and usually a cold, insipid partner, a poor, neglectful mother or father. But if this line has a sister line, that is, a small line running parallel with the Girdle, it argues intemperance and lust in both sexes and baseness in sexual matter; a filthy person. If this line be divided or broken up by various lines, it denotes losses and infamy by reason of these lusts.

The Line of Mars. Courage and Fortitude

This line is sometimes called the sister line to the line of Life because it is often found running parallel with that line and denotes increased vital force; courage, because it strengthens the heart and thus the energy. When clear and well-defined it presages a long and active life, with little or no diseases. People with this line will suffer largely from gout, rheumatism and apoplexy if they take stimulants of any kind, inasmuch as the person will have sufficient energy of himself, and all stimulation which will increase the vascular action will only impede and retard the heart's action, like too much oil to a machine. This line strengthens all things denoted by the line of Life, and if clear and decidedly red, it promises great success in war.

The Rule to Tell the Planets

When a figure similar to that used by astronomers in designating the planets is found on the mount particularly set aside for that planet, as on the mount of Jupiter there is the figure ♃, and on the mount of Saturn there is the sign ♄, on Apollo the sign ☉, on the mount of Mercury there is the sign ☿, and on the thick part of the thumb you find a similar sign ♀, on the mount of the moon the sign ☽, on Mars' place the figure ♂, and so on, then they are termed benevolent. How far, however, this is relevant to the subject I do not state, but I should rather advise the student to treat this with great care, although the marks given underneath will be found of value when placed as indicated.

The planets are considered unfortunate when confused lines, broken semicircle, gridiron marks, or signs contrary to the mounts indicated above, as ♃ to mount of Jupiter, and so on, are found on the mounts or places.

Venus (♀) is dignified when you find on her mount a clear star, or red furrows running transversely parallel.

A jovial, merry nature is shown by fullness or elevation of the root of the thumb, but luxurious, amorous, graceful, comely, concupiscent, very honest, just and constant in friendship.

Description when strong and full: the body somewhat tall, skin clear, eyes pleasant and sparkling, full of allurement and temptation. The hair is brown, light, crisp and soft, sometimes slightly waving in front or curling; a noble mind. The mind is ofttimes prone to boasting, and loves the society of ladies; an admirer of music, painting and beauty.

Profession must be judged according to the strength or debility of the mount; it produces musicians, merchants for fancy goods, teachers, apothecaries, gardeners, etc.

The mount weak, not elevated or badly marked, cause men to be inconstant, lascivious and vain. A cross near first joint of the thumb signifies an adulterer, or has had or will have a mishap through females.

The place of Venus, void of incisures, flat and smooth-looking, shows and effeminate, rude and sorrowful person, or one foolishly and ridiculously addicted to merriment and jesting.

The Planet Mars. Courage, War

Mars is fortunate (1) when line of Life is strong, deep, red and decently drawn; (2) when a cross or star is found on his place, especially the palm of the hand.

Description when strong: denotes full courage, often bold, dauntless, stout, warlike, contentious, firm of purpose, large and lusty appetite, imperious.

Hair light brown or sandy, yellow, often red.

The eyes, blue or grey-green, which often grow red and terrible-looking when angry.

Mars unfortunate: men, etc., are quarrelsome, violent, deceitful, angry natures; produces thieves and murderers.

Profession according to strength: generals, surgeons, ironmasters or workers and tradesmen of all kinds who work with metal, as ironmongers, farriers, etc.

Note – Mars has signification of wives, husbands, sons and friends (deceitful or otherwise).

Diseases: produces fevers, blisters, sore eyes, skin diseases, apoplexy, wounds, and wicked thoughts.

With Jupiter, he affects the privy parts and sexual diseases.

If Mars be strong, females have largely constructed bodies and love men of rank; if Venus be storng, men love women of rank; if weak they form attachments for servants, coachmen and inferiors.

The sign ♄ placed in cavea of the hand threatens a fall from a precipice or some high place; a fall is also indicated by the line of Saturn stopping or breaking on the mount of Mars (hollow of hand).

Imprisonment: a crooked line ascending from mount of Mars to the mount of Saturn.

Journeys and peregrinations denoted by a line running from plain of Mars (hollow of hand) down to the Bracelet lines and ending immediately below the mount of the Moon.

The Mount of Jupiter. Honour, Fame, Renown, Ecclesiastical, State, Law

The planet is fortunate when (1) a star or double cross, (2) parallel lines or (3) line clearly drawn from line of Life to his mount.

Description when fortunate: he signifies a noble, glorious, honest, benevolent, affable, honourable, merry, renowned, neat, just and equitable person; good-looking, formidable and happy, with beautiful hazel or blue eyes.

Hair dark brown; grave gesture, modest, and faithful to their promises.

Professions: great dignitaries, churchmen, lawyers or counsellors, statesmen or persons brought into contact with great men who are highly esteemed and loved. They favour their wives, sons, and all good men.

Jupiter rules the liver, blood, ribs, lungs and gristles.

Jupiter unfortunate when half a gridiron on his mount. This shows losses by powerful women. When generally unfortunate: when flat, flabby, with no good marks on it, interlaced with a lot of little hair lines, etc., he causes persons to lose their estates and brings about great calamities in money matters. Although, if nothing else stops it, the person will usually recover it after he becomes strong.

Diseases: when afflicted he causes troubles of the heart, cramps, inflammation of the lungs, windy spasms.

Apoplexy indicated by a line transversely cutting his mount and extending towards the mount of Saturn (middle finger), and forming there a cleft or little lines.

Splendid honours and fame, riches, public rewards from princes and great men, a cross, especially a clear and red star on the mount of Jupiter of ♃ marked thereon.

The Mount of Apollo. The Planet Sun. Ingenuity, Public Honours, Brilliancy

The Sun is fortunate: same as in last planet.

Description when fortunate: persons are faithful, ingenious, honoured, high-minded, wise, humane, religious, just, moderate, aged, and do all things wisely.

He gives a well-set body with yellow or sandy hair, and rules the heart and eyes, the diaphragm (bowels) and nerves.

Description when unfortunate: the persons are proud and easily elated, manifesting their access to dignity by unjust means, boasters and immodest.

Diseases: he produces sore eyes and blindness, especially of right eye in a man and left in a woman, and trembling of the heart, syncope, etc.

Political honours: the Via Solis being uniform and of a clear good colour; it also gives the favour and grace of princes.

Trouble and enmity from political and legal men when the Via Solis is confused and afflicted.

The Moon. Travelling by Land and Sea

When fortunate: good and clear marks near this mount, stars, etc. These persons are successful in journeys and messages and great prosperity in foreign countries; to a female, felicity and happiness in bearing children.

Ominous signs placed here show death and affliction in childbirth.

Description: the persons will be famous, honest and honourable, with well-set large bodies proportioned and pleasant. They travel by land and sea, and causes them to desire to lie or walk by the side of water – rivers and running waters.

When unfortunate, principally known by pale and confused line on the mount of the Moon.

The mount flat, soft and small, she causes persons to be inconstant in life and actions.

Diseases: affects the brain, stomach and belly, and occasions paralysis, epilepsy, cancer, spots on the body, gripings and severe colds.

The Planet Saturn. The Mount of Saturn. Counsels, Mathematicians, Grave Thinkers, Inventors

When fortunate: when the line of Saturn runs uniformly and clear to his mount of ♄ marked thereon.

Saturn unfortunate when there are confused lines on his mount or contrary or unfortunate signs thereon.

Saturn fortunate: men are silent, provident; good and profound, not always rich, counsels, grave meditators, somewhat melancholy, and generally have a foolish way of laughing and jesting.

Description: they generally have a slender body, and are rather tall, pale and feeble.

Hair brown or blackish in colour, yet sometimes sandy. The eyes are sunken.

Trades, etc.: they are fortunate in agriculture, in minerals of all kinds, as mines, etc. They are somewhat careless of their wives and less addicted to sexual excesses, are more grasping and tenacious than is just.

When Saturn is unfortunate he makes persons sorrowful, laborious, sordid, humble, covetous, unfaithful, liars, unfortunate, malicious, oppressed with continual griefs and calamities.

Diseases: he gives dangerous diseases, colds, coughs, melancholy, hypochondriacal complaints, dropsy, gout, falling sickness, quartan and hectic fevers.

Accidents: he produces falls from houses, imprisonment and danger of drowning.

A deep line running from the space between the forefinger and middle finger to the line of Fortune and cutting or interrupting it, signifies a wound or disease in the lower part of the abdomen.

The Planet Mercury. The Mount of Mercury. Study, Research, Sciences, Speaking

When this planet is fortunate, men are ingenious, studious, scientific and searchers after secrets.

Professions, trades, etc., according to his dignity: he produces orators, poets, eloquent speakers, persons ready to learn anything, mathematicians, merchants; sometimes crafty, variable people.

When unfortunate, he produces persons full of levity, liars, prattlers, thieves, cheats, inconstant, faithless, traitors, etc.

Diseases: he produces madness, fury, acute fevers, etc.

Signs of deceit and danger to life; the mensa sharpened by the conscourse of the line of Fortune and the line of Life or the Liver line. The best sign is the mensa diverging, open at both ends and forming the figure >—<

Perfection of wit and science: a star placed (or other clearly-formed flowers or flag) in the mensa, especially under the mount of Mercury or the Sun.

Mensa. The Part of Fortune

When fortunate: liberal, magnanimous and long-lived people. The space between the line of Fortune and the Liver line (sometimes called the line of the Heart and the line of the Head), and forms a nice figure.

When unfortunate: small and narrow (by the approaching of these two lines), it argues slender fortune, niggardliness and fearfulness.

Honours and dignities to follow by great and noble personages, when a star or cross appears in this space, clear and well-formed, especially under the mount of the Sun (see chapter on figures and flower on hand).

The sign of ♃ here promises prominent ecclesiastical dignities.

Good fortune is denoted by the star or triple cross. Good and equal lines in this space denote a good fortune; evil or unequal lines, the reverse.

The worst sign when no mensa is found, for it shows obscurity both of life and fortune.

Misfortune and loss of honours when confused little lines appear here, the good is diverted, and anxieties and troubles threaten, to honours especially, if under the mount of the Sun.

Fortunate journeys; a cross or star on the outermost part of the mensa on or near the mount of the Moon is a sure sign.

Riches and honours shown by overthwart lines clear and red underneath the nail and joint of the thumb.

A violent death or danger through a married woman, etc.: a line passing from the upper joint of the thumb to the line of Life.

A contentious nature: confused lines on the lower joint of the thumb; on always brawling and scolding.

Riches and possessions – to be worked for: equal furrows under the lower joint.

Idleness and lack of energy: if the first and second joints are void of incisures.

The Forefinger or Index Finger

Inheritance: denoted by many overthwart lines in the top joint; these in the second joint show evious and evil-disposed persons.

Issue, bad tongue: right line running between the top and second joints declare in a woman a numerous issue; in a man bitterness of tongue.

A jovial disposition: right lines in the joint near the mount of Jupiter.

Unchaste and lascivious: in a female hand a star being placed in the joint near the mount of Jupiter.

An unhappy, melancholy and depraved mind: denoted by small gridirous or confused marks in the joints of this finger.

Success with metals: manifested by equal line.

Drowning or violent death: this is denoted by a star in the joints of this finger.

Folly and madness: a crossed line, extending from the root of this finger upwards through the whole length of the finger.

The Ring Finger

Great and noble fame denoted by a line ascending unbroken from the mount of the Sun through the joints of this finger to the end.

Honour and riches: this is shown by equal lines in the first joint (near the mount).

Enmity of great men: denoted by overthwart lines here; it is made late in life when these lines are intersected.

The Little Finger

The planet Mars has dominion over this finger. A strong and valorous person when strong and well fed.

Note – From the joints of this finger as from the mount itself are judgments passed concerning merchandise and favours.

Ingenuity and eloquence: a star in the first joint (near the mount of Mercury) shows this; it is also shown by a right line extending from the mount of Mercury to the end of finger, also a great speaker.

Foolishness, etc., denoted by obtuse and confused marks placed here.

A thief and deceitful person: this is shown by confused and unfortunate marks appearing in the first and second joints of this finger.

Perpetual inconstancy: this is shown by adverse lines in the last or top joint of the finger.

Note – The number of wives and husbands are frequently indicated from the small lines passing from the outermost part of the hand to the mount of Mercury, but I consider the proper place is from the mount of Venus.

If the end of the little finger does not reach so far as to touch the last joint of the ring finger, it signifies that the partner in marriage will be imperious in all things.

The mounts marked with good figures and characters show good and happy omens, being vitiated with confused or broken characters, etc., or lines, they always denote the contrary, unless they are restrained by other lines that be good.

Cheiromancers generally teach that the first joints near the mount of the finger indicate the early age; the second, the flourishing state of manhood; and the last old age. But our opinion is that the planets shown by the nativity of the persons do, in their proper order, manifest their marks and characters, whether for good or bad.

Note – A knowledge of astrology will prove an acquisition to the study of palmistry or any science.

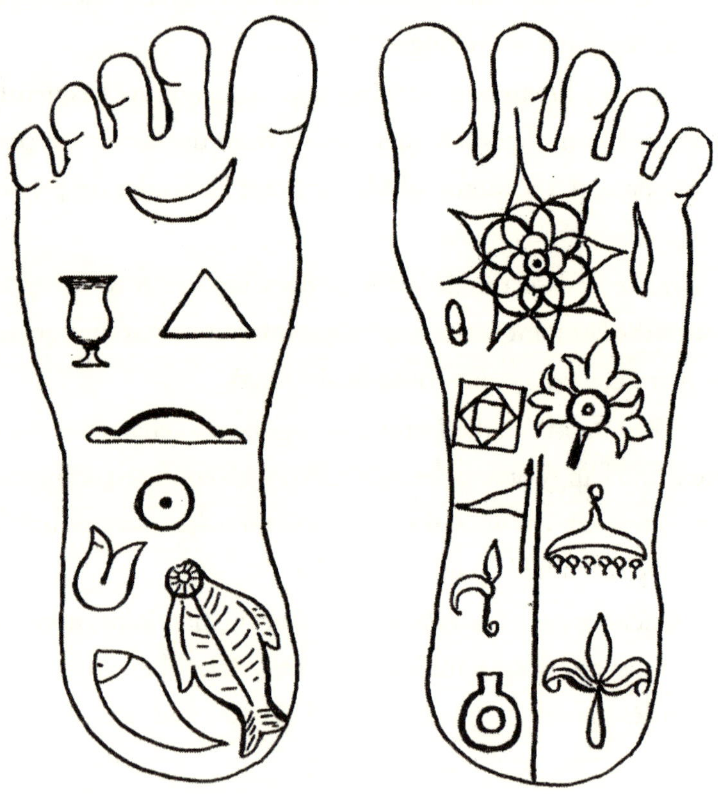

Alleged marks on the feet of the benign Buddha

Signs on the Head. How to Read the forehead

If a person has a broad forehead and takes the form of ⌒, a crescent, he was born of poor parents but is sure to be rich.

If a prominent single vein or mark extends from the nose to the top of the forehead the person is born to immense wealth.

If there are many similarly placed, the person is very vicious.

If the forehead is depressed in the middle he is very jealous and a lascivious or sinful man.

If the forehead is narrow, he is a great miser.

If there be three furrows going across the head, he is likely to live a long life, especially if they go over the eyes.

If there be four such lines, the person will be a commander or great potentate and live a very long time.

Many indistinct lines on the forehead denote lewd persons.

If there be any marks in the middle of the forehead and they take the form of a crescent ⌒, the person will be very prosperous and fortunate.

Signs on the Feet

If a crescent or elongated horseshoe mark appears on sole of the foot and the toes separated well from each other, the person will have a harsh temper and remain poor.

If a female's toes are well set together and close, and has a wheel or flower mark on either or both feet, she will become a lady of rank and position.

If there be an ear-shaped figure on the foot and without hair, or a little tuft, the person may expect to be successful in the world.

The Arms

If her arms are very long, she will be renowned and well-to-to. Short-armed persons generally remain poor.